POETRY BY GAVIN BANTOCK

Juggernaut

A New Thing Breathing

Eirenikon

Anhaga
(SIX POEMS FROM THE ANGLO-SAXON)

Dragons

Floating World

Just Think of It

GAVIN BANTOCK

SeaManShip

A USER'S MANUAL

Nine Configurations

ANVIL PRESS POETRY

Published in 2003
by Anvil Press Poetry Ltd
Neptune House 70 Royal Hill London SE10 8RF
www.anvilpresspoetry.com

Copyright © Gavin Bantock 2003

ISBN 0 85646 358 2

This book is published
with financial assistance from
The Arts Council of England

A catalogue record for this book
is available from the British Library

The moral rights of the author have been asserted in
accordance with the Copyright, Designs and Patents Act 1988

Designed and set in Monotype Columbus by Anvil
Printed and bound in England
by Cromwell Press, Trowbridge, Wiltshire

CONTENTS

READ ME FIRST   9

I   *Sea*

    Start Up   13
    Desktop   23
    Install   33

II   *Man*

    Open   45
    Enter   55
    Edit   65

III   *Ship*

    Save   77
    Print   87
    Shut Down   97

GLOSSARY   107

TO THE SHINING YOUNG

READ ME FIRST

For more than twenty years, I had been attempting to compose a poem to be called "SeaManShip", which made use of the three elements in the word – "sea" to represent the natural world; "man" the human intellect, and "ship", man's inventions or the so-called artificial world. The poem was to be a kind of manifesto, a statement of what I believe. I made many false starts. From the beginning, in 1975, I knew the poem would be in three parts; I knew it would make much of the number three, and I knew it would in some way make use of rhyme. The overriding problem was to find a suitable form.

In April 1996, I scribbled out a poem called "Memory" (in *Just Think of It*, page 48). It linked a very old poem about a golden ram which I wrote when I was a teenager with the RAM (random access memory) of my Macintosh computer. A few days later, while re-working this poem and while again searching for a form for *SeaManShip*, it occurred to me to cast the latter loosely in the form of a computer manual. I found nine basic processes necessary when using a word-processor, and starting with my most recent attempt, I began to write this long poem with new intensity. It took several weeks to work out the rhyme scheme and line arrangement and to dovetail the older material into the new form, but once that was achieved I forged ahead and finished the first complete draft on 13th July, 1996.

The poem is not really a manual and it certainly does not express all of my so-called "philosophy", although it is largely autobiographical. Much of the computer language and use of the manual form might seem superficial, but I did find an extraordinarily rich source of new words and expressions in the jargon of the computer world, and I think I have produced a manifesto of a kind, even if it is not usable as such.

Gavin Bantock

I *Sea*

Start Up

Starting up from the shutdown
window of the mainframe
    SEA,
a pixel bit of quicktime seed shot upstart from the crammed
gonad of the god of white waters and grew brave into gremlin
    MAN,
whose burning drive to upgrade the blueprints of his dreams has now
trashed the thalassa chains with his virused devices and terminating
    SHIP.
And I, called up to monitor the unbuttoned power of the current,
prompted from the screen the wild eep I thought of a virgin merman's
    glee
at his first coming, and saw, strung whitehaired out in the grayscale
deep, the ghosted image of his onan milk fade to a mere
    blip
of erased souls in the running glasnost of the coldwar ocean.
And booted up by this revelation of eros genesis and death I then
    began
a staged process, like a showboat's maiden journey long delayed,
to define and play out my own thalassinos role in the trackball
    trip
across the crashed motherboards of the spanking world.
And powered-up by the random cache of memory, I know that if first I
    can
helm the lost ark of seamanship to the destination port of the hereafter,
I will a little have fulfilled the multifinder task assigned, I believe, to
    me.

The SEA, I have since found, the macro of nature, formats
the total earthworld of our blue-pearl disk-space,
>   and
have found that MAN is alone the searching mind that nests
the iconed folders of the cosmos, and have found too that
>   each
and every SHIP is an emblem of everything
lovely or slovenly ever
>   made
with his hands – whether it be the rammed windscreens of stratojets
or the radial mirror-balls he's fired from the shellshocked
>   sand,
or whether the passacaglia swells of organ thunder
shuddering through his gigalith cathedrals, or the filigree
>   braid
laid comely on the brow of a camelot queen, or even
a backbroken cruiser spewing oil on a gulled
>   beach.
For ours I have found is a time where
these crafted argosies of man's imaginaton
>   invade
and jason every chaste creek of the chastened Earth;
and also in time where man himself, craving now only to
>   reach
something less than a paradise, will become little more
than a throbbing venereal aqueous
>   gland.

Or I say, for my singular self in the first person,
the sea is that dashing tundra of god that
        inspires
all that ever I do, and for me likewise man is
the union incarnation of all
        those
I have ever loved or loved me, and every ship is
a memorandum of all the seafaring
        tales
filed in the logbook of the journeys I have lifelong made.
The laced waves have thus assumed the roles of alias
        lyres
played by the wind. And the singing young,
like the blue-eyed descryings of distant
        sails,
people the wetland dreams of my wanderlust,
and in every scurrilous ocean gale that
        crows
I hear the voiced annotations of anguish,
mine and theirs, and though the incontinent
        wails
of gulls fill me thereafter with renewed longings,
the foreglimpse of joy, unattained,
        grows
unbearably lovely and serves there
only to whiplash the nerve-ends of my unsatisfied
        desires.

I so much need to configure ways to escape from
this hoarse chorale of the brash
    SEA,
which ruthlessly undertows my freaked mind
with its incessant dirge for plaintext
    MAN.
As if I seem, spotlit on the lowest rung of a liner
companionway, to be lost in the cerebrum hold of a steel
    SHIP
that's unwilling, unable perhaps, to boldface horizons
and chart me a course to run down the wind and sail
    free
from this struck-through italic life on land
that holds me fast in a numlocked
    grip
that's more, oh, so much more tungsten than virtual
or cold reality. And yet, were I free, I would find I
    can
never make headway enough
from the taloned clutch of the land's decorum to
    rip
out the anchored icons, create and enter a new
and a clean paradise, unburdened beyond the fixed
    meridian
pagebreak of my numbered days, from the fernfresh
gem of the first water to the trickling dry cascade of burial
    scree.

Scant hope for me then, as I scan and catch the drift,
landlocked and iconoclast as I am, to
>   thrive
long a longshoreman or stand firm on any shore long,
unless I conform and confirm and wordperfectly
>   understand
first exactly what the shining fused sea is,
how it formed and fashioned the centred
>   source,
the headstream of shimmering earth-life,
and how what stays here stays here and stays
>   alive;
and learn also exactly what the frail-skinned
man I am is, and what seamanlike
>   force
drives me to find and to find
refuge in places beyond the terminal
>   land,
and what mad or what sane godheads within
or above or elsewhere lay out my outlined
>   course;
and unless also, I can handcraft
a ship, unwreckable,
>   manned
too with a crew reckless enough
to do more than merely
>   survive.

I can, I suppose, never
comprehend what the tritoned sea means,
     except
by the trite means of knowing
the parts of its sum. It is easy
     enough
to glean facts, to index, perhaps,
the marine catalogue, to
     assess
how long nine grains of salt
might undissolved be
     kept
crystal in a shellful of sea,
or, more highbrow, to
     impress
others with the names of every
oceangoing galleon:
     stuff
lexicons reek of; but stuffed wordbooks, now matter
how splendid the bindings are, are so much
     less
inspiring than the silver-lined wine-dark spines and vital
blue covers of the sea, and bound within them, its gentle,
     rough
bullions, its deepest chasms
where no man yet has ever
     stepped.

Nor, I find, can I mine much
deeper down or deep enough into the veined
      mind
of mankind, for, in vain, however much
I come to know, I never know
      why
I know it, or know why I have come here,
learning how little I have come to
      know.
I sometimes stand hovering on a hawking
brink of understanding, only to
      find
the flash of instinct, that big-bang dream,
fading into a dull
      glow
of animal wonder; as if all
sparks of eureka genius darken and
      die
the very moment they might be
about to ignite and
      rainbow
round in a sunburst of radiant flowers;
and then I drizzledroop down and
      sigh
oh, childlike at a window, at the loss of
something shadow-like just
      behind.

We've built real ships, aye, schooners,
coracles, and, aye aye, steel oracles of
        space,
but all seagoings go nowhere
truly newer than where they
        began,
or, aye, are soon broken under breakers;
and those that brave the black
        slipstream
cyber of the spinning stars journey back sometimes,
having found no other
        place
friendly in the limbo galaxies.
What ship I've built from the breakthrough
        dream
of desiring to know
decays like the dream itself: no
        artisan
ever yet has designed
a splendent masterpiece that will still
        gleam
brightly at the far end of time;
and no work of giant or humdrum
        man
is godlike enough
not to erode away without a
        trace.

SEAMANSHIP, the supreme knowhow of living best a-sea,
I once believed that sailing men once
      knew,
evades me, it seems, forever, has become
a built-in skill I can, any of me,
      never
retrieve the more I acquire it,
as if I spin and tumble within a child's
      balloon,
that, as it expands, creates
a greater known knowable
      view
of the unknown outside itself;
a moist pupa inside a half hyaline
      cocoon
that dreams of but never
sees the petalkiss angel it will
      endeavour
to become; knowing though that
the bright day, oh, will start up
      soon,
but wondering about what wings are,
and wondering too how
      ever
they will lift their little, light, leaden weight into
the wingless realms of burdenless
      blue.

Desktop

Nevertheless, I dare, I will dare, have
dared to learn ways to
      sail,
to manual the known sea-crafts,
to turn, to lectern, to collect what after all is only a
      dream
into a cached chalice I can touch and
cherish, hope with, hold and
      keep
with me forever, and then
bequeathe to others, so that if I
      fail
to linger here long enough,
someone perhaps can somehow
      peep
through a keyhole of my masterpiece
and in a rogue
      beam
of sunshine in that room
beyond the door, slant into my tilded
      sleep
to catch an inkling of the song,
or a precious fragment of its scrolled
      theme,
and thereafter perhaps hold
wholly my holy long-lost
      grail.

I have master-patterned the living
desktops of young minds for thirty
    years,
and when, as they do often, they have
ever asked me how I am able to
    find
verve and panache enough at my age to stay so much
further ahead in the vanguard than they are and keep my eyes
    ablaze,
I tell them, oh, that the glistening trustlights in *their* eyes,
brim-bright and micro-planeted with real
    tears,
not only the tristesse in them but the laughter also,
have always mirrored for me – what is it? – oh, the exultant
    sprays
scattered windward and flamboyant from the sea's ebullient
constellations; which themselves, though seemingly
    blind,
rekindle in me the maestro, the celestial fires that rage
across the nightscapes and stampede through the blustering
    days,
and so regalvanize the iron of – aye, fascinate anew
the untameable maelstrom of – my gyro-driven
    mind,
a thing to them of such charisma, inspiring such love they tell me,
that they too resolve to become, like me, horizon-assassinating
    pioneers.

The sea, then, the eyes of the young,
these both, seeming to see
        all
but not understanding,
give me the strength to give
        them
the will to want to know well
themselves — what they can
        do,
what god-given gifts they have got,
what voices will
        call
them to the mountains,
what chooser nuances of inkjet
        blue
they will paint the birds
they hark after, what
        jerusalem
will be their city,
when the gods come marching
        through
to fascinate their minds with
jewels of thought, and what
        gem
will be their supreme birthstone before they,
unedened, aye, unedened,
        fall.

Aye, unedened – for like a stately island
surrounded by the round sea, a minaret
    land
beckoning the young, and disney blue
sky and snowwhite clouds in my pasted
    smile,
I liken myself to a god, a kindly
haven, harbouring what seem to be
    sublime
seacraft docked in the slipway
corners of my eyes, ships which I confess now, yes, are
    manned,
though, with battened down crews of harridan
backslash lusts, on red alert for a real
    time
command to sail out into the still
waters of their souls, which all the
    while,
oh, trust me to teach them the angel walkways.
Teetering, therefore, tiptoe from
    crime,
I gather them into my arms and, true to tell,
tell them I too love them – while, at the same time,
    paedophile
imaginings and inarticuate longings
flood into my heart like golden
    contraband.

Yet the sea is my salvation.
A control, strong as the stallion
>   tides
that govern oceans, always reins me back
and gags the pent volcanoes. No tidal
>   waves
have yet thundered out of me or broken them.
An adamantine commandant
>   dwells
ermined among the silicone columns of my kinglike
brain, lines the inner
>   sides
of my innermost atman,
and clangs like an insane carambole of cuestruck
>   bells,
warning me to thrust my gargoyle longings
stillborn down into still
>   graves,
so that my wisdom-lullabye
voice of love never
>   tells
its true story, and they are saved.
It is the sea that
>   saves
them; as with them with me also:
it is the sea that
>   guides.

Thus has the honest sea's self kept me
the self-styled dishonest guru I am, a marginal
    saint
hunched like a snivelling goblin clerk punching at random
keys on the console desk in his crypted cell beneath high vaulted
    halls
that echo then with his piped and consoling hamelin
anthems the young, oh, so achingly long to
    sing;
and there too, under white-sky moulded ceilings,
I hang my rows of gilt-framed oils, the gaudy
    paint
of which conceals abomination
as pretty as a jellyfish's
    sting,
that, oozing as wounds do, would run rancid
like slow whale oil down the stained and flaking damask
    walls,
were it not that my merged respect for the sea
and for these, aye, these tyro midshipmen, induces me to
    bring
them rather to a paradise of knowing
so beautiful it utterly
    appals
even the angels, who, once having seen it, die;
an eden coined after, not before, the first
    taint.

Just as the sea,
from which all greenhorn vitality first
    emerged,
now lockers the world's garbage,
yet still has the guts to
    create
pure rains, freshly distilled,
to fall kindly on the thirsting
    ground.
Which is to say again – that not only life,
but death also,
    surged
splendid and leapt singing from
the ocean in that first-born outward
    bound;
and, also, that all the lily-whites of love
bloom from the dragon seeds of dragdown
    hate.
Thus, nurturing saplings,
a greenweed longing to
    confound
goes hand in hand with
the emerald ambition, oh, somehow to
    educate.
Thus I lay out the patterns, user-friendly, of my own desktop,
from the semblant beauty of which no flaws can ever be
    purged.

Which is to say in the end that a true
teacher of men cannot and need not have to
      be
a paragon of goodness,
and that the most pure mahatman
      christ
has to acknowledge, if ever
he walks the earth in humankindly
      form,
that the leanings of anatomy
will never leave him or set him
      free
from the stuffed folders of procreation,
even if the burning sleet and hail mary
      storm
and shingles of a wet daydream may be ignored.
The pulpit-addicted priests profess that God
      sacrificed
his only begotten Son for mankind, but
that need not ever mean that the boldfaced
      warm
risings of the frocked flesh were a cloud-nine nine-day
beatitude that Jesus Christ denied. Surely he too was
      enticed
by the seventh-veil heaven of a woman or a boy's nudity
no less than you, or no less, indeeed, than a man like
      me.

Lucifer was, and still is,
beautiful; the filthiest serial
    homicide
can weave the most delicate
posies to hand smiling to a little
    girl,
and even kiss her on the lips,
without a pixel dribble of lust or leering
    guilt.
Even the fluid stools of a pig
can prime a rose with blushing
    pride,
and innocent minnows
clean their scales in poisoned
    silt;
just as the elephant-man of the oyster
hones in its roughcast crust a cloned
    pearl.
And though I may foster
sword-like thinkings to the uttermost
    hilt,
I go always the buckram way of the sea,
and stress, in a non-stop white-noise
    swirl,
that this is the me I am, and that each wave that breaks
shells on the seashore is, in some way is, somehow always is,
    justified.

Install

In the beginning was the Word,
and the Word was with God, and the Word was, well, rather
>soft.
And the same was in the beginning with God
when first he installed it in the highstreet hardware
>store
somewhere along the sea front; for the Word was
a swarming plague of bugs and glitched bytes – and God
>stalled.
And I find now I have no option: I cannot shift the command
elsewhere, and cannot control the Word to send it
>aloft
back to the Gates of heaven, for when Eve bit knowingly into
Adam's apple of knowhow, all Eden was instantly
>walled
round with the fractal holograms of chaos,
and there was no craft to escape in from that contoured
>shore.
So I sit here now at a manual of keys but with no power
to reboot the powerbook of God, yet have I believe been
>called
forth to isaiah the new server of the kingdom.
But when I lifted up mine eyes to the heavens to
>implore
for help and inspiration, all I heard was a nervous
fluttering of wings, and someone I think up there merely
>coughed.

So I looked north and saw Woden, one-eyed and hatless,
lying jewelled in a funeral ship about to be sent
>   out
aflame into the Wednesday midnight sun,
and I looked south and I saw the solar ship of hieroglyphed
>   Ra
irradium down from the sky to the sphinx underworld
but not again come up to reinstall him on the primeval
>   hill.
And I looked east and I saw the nine imperial dragons
locked in the red compound of the forbidden city, a chessboard
>   redoubt
where Buddha was banned and abandoned. So I looked west,
but the gods there were all knaves and the gambling popes were
>   still
waiting for the last trump, and I looked up again to the heavens
but all I could see was the swansong of a bloodshot shooting
>   star.
And on the ground the words of all the world's books
lay scattered like leaves, and I knew then I must summon up the
>   will
somehow from now to roget a new thesaurus, attempt to restore
the deleted files of the past and erase the disfiguring
>   scar
from the dragged down face of God. But I had no means, and
no means of knowing how, oh, how to bring this total overhaul
>   about.

But I thought if I went out with a clipboard and picked up
whatever art I could clip from the littered courtyard
      stones,
I might have the skill to compile a kind of holy scrapbook
or paste together a boat of paper
      leaves,
and programme a journey through the waterless
white horses in the wilderness of flawed
      words,
and perhaps find a new island and build a city there that
would never crash into ruins or end up an ezekiel of dry
      bones;
and if I could I would origami all the remaining
pages and set them up into perfect formations of flying
      birds,
that would, like the rainbow and the dove, promise
a peace between God and man so that neither ever
      grieves
again. Then perhaps heaven would have the courage to send us
a new Word or a Word perfect or a Word future so that even the
      surds
that jinx science and the breathed sounds of phonetics
would find a voice and become for the first time rational
      breves
beeped out by God, that might be at last correctly installed
in the established mainframes of the world and all their
      clones.

But words rust and grow redundant like the daisy
wheels of flowers, are cunningly foxed, or chameleon their
> sounds;
so the snatching yester claws of *wyrd* have gone to the dogs
with clipped nails – a weirdo deviation; and radiant *love*, that once
> expressed
the true brotherhood of round tables or a tristan zenith,
is sold now as a candied valentine or the titillations of a simpering
> tart.
The newest thesaurus is half-a-dinosaur old the moment it appears
on a station bookstall, and the runes found carved in Celtic burial
> mounds
cannot be decoded; and *surf,* I once believed was the way to spell
the voices of waves, is now re-verbed in a skintight wavetop
> art,
or's a mode of browsing through the webs of data spun out in
the sizzling galaxies of the internet – and the crying gulls have gone
> west.
Latterday bards have disrobed, become baud-crazed poetasters
with no taste for words in any tongue. It's now time for them to
> restart
the engines of invention and find new ways to make old words
reactivate the glossaries of the past, and to recoin the
> best
kennings possible in a world where language has almost lost
its skill to express true feelings and the human voice no longer
> astounds.

And numbers also: if you or I had eleven fingers and three hands,
we might never think of the nine muses in the same way, and the
    eight
tentacles of an octopus might somehow seem odd, and a week
perhaps not have seven days, and the six sides of a lucky-strike
    die
might be refaced with a bean and a half, plus one point five of one,
plus a bean and fifty percent of another, and half a
    bean,
and both five and six be the middle point of an asymmetric code.
We might even not even be able to conceive of even as a euclid
    state
where even two odd sides are equal. But there would still be four
winds, and God could still be three in one, and it would
    mean,
too, that the seventh wave could still exceed the other six.
There could still be sixty seconds in each of the sixty minutes, and
    pi
could still be the sixteenth letter of Greek or the ratio of circle
to circumference. But, indeed, if we are ever to keep
    green
the Tree of Knowledge and re-install the Word re-worded
after putting right what is left of Eden, we must first
    try
to upgrade all the high ends from behemoth to iota, and keep them
alive, like bright blue bearings spinning forever on a white
    plate.

And bearing that in mind, I'm somewhat consoled to know that
man stands at the fulcrum of known macro and micro, yet if there's
> mind
in the pixel of a quark or beyond the event horizons of black holes,
I wonder then if there's wit there to conceive of size in the selfsame
> way,
or whether perhaps we have to einstein the idea of one stone only:
that the boulder moon and a grain of sand are simply one and the
> same.
Or question whether in the possible universe there is as much light
as dark, or whether there is more discovered than there is to
> find,
or whether the frozen realms of the Dis underworld
contain as much ice as exists in the blaze of a comet's
> flame,
or whether even sleep would be necessary if there were no night
and we lived wide awake and weatherworn in one perpetual
> day.
I sometimes think that one night God picked up a pack of wild
cards and flung them into the sky and the next day failed to
> tame
them; and yet, when at times I've denied godhead beyond myself,
I find that a certain psyche must have designed the liquid crystal
> display
of a melting snowflake; and I know I could access the entire
system of the cosmos if I knew where that imagesetting Driver was
> enshrined.

Thus what to begin with becomes the very end I aim at,
and my resolution is this: that in the beginning I'm the white
      page
of a red cross knight who sets sail across the black disk of the sea,
and that all I need to do is cross my heart that I will blindly
      serve
my mounted master without ever asking what or who he is.
Then, when he turns his face for the first time, maybe I'll see him
      smile;
for there is unquestionably a joy in being infinitely patient
when the alternative might be to kindle only the sea-captain's
      rage.
There is joy too in carrying a warrior's shield and sword
and knowing that I may never need to use them, and this will
      reconcile
me to the absence of honour in inaction: for the responsibility
to win wars is not mine, and to win fame may not be what I
      deserve.
A manual is made for whatever is new, and its wisdom is derived
from whatever is old, and the whole world walks in a single
      file
in the wake of knights in the cavalcade of days; and if I wish to be
installed in a sound caravanserai on the searoad, I must have the
      nerve
to remain silent until I learn what it means to be – and how I might
one day myself become – a knight errant commander of reverend
      age.

But this earth, this resplendent castle I live in,
glowworm warm along the roaring
    shore,
has irresistible charisma,
which is why so often I
    resign
myself to the chandelier
charms of banquet-chambers ablaze with utopian
    gold,
those gorgeous, tapestry-laden rooms
shining with fountains and the aurora fonts of faeryland
    lore,
folklore and folk that never fail to enchant me,
and, oh, rambling charters of law also, that always
    hold
me bit-champing back, stall me, confine me,
and keep me from trying any more to
    define
the Word and find the words of that unfound legend,
so new, aye, new, yet so refreshingly
    old,
that I hear, aye, hear always, in that one unattainable
room, a song so delectable, so ineffably
    divine,
that not even God or any left of the living gods,
if ever they heard it, can hear it any
    more.

I live here, aye, I cry out, but what's more bootless, more unheard
or more unheard-of, than hammering clavier thunder in an empty
      hall?
For too long I have been feeding off the fatbits of the land,
abandoning to others the things that I myself should have
      done.
It's so easy to quit, or to condemn the achievements of mankind,
to sit back and say I could have done better with a battering
      ram.
I should be scorned for having done so little to help the hackers tunnel
through the brainwave darkness of the unknown, the impenetrable
      wall
of enigma thicker than the stacked manuals of innumerable Words;
should be scourged for taking so little seriously and not giving a
      damn!
The task before us is to customize and dedicate our robotic steeds
and spur them on furioso towards the driven disk of the hard
      sun.
Stand up, then, and drag down the shining icons of *SeaManShip*
or somehow *phasmanise* them and thus merge them into a serial
      anagram!
Give *an emphasis* to the *main shapes* and *main phases* of the given
program, that's become such *a misshapen* application it cannot now be
      run!
Or, better still, coin easy munchausen freewares called *ManaPheSis,*
SenAsaPhim, or *PanMesSiah,* say, that even a blindfold dingbat could
      install!

11   *Man*

Open

Open ye the gates, whoever knocks. Or: *Open, locks,*
that the righteous nation that keepeth the truth may enter
        in.
Or rather: *Afoot and light-hearted I take to the open road,*
healthy, free, the world before me, leading wherever I
        choose.
Or if not — *The untented cosmos my abode, I pass,*
a willful stranger, my mistress still the open
        road.
False beginnings: such litmus lines are random baptists of past
openings; and crying in the cyberness double-quick to
        begin,
I twice clicked the icon precursor of x.y.z. to access
the A.B.C. of the Word, and waited, watching the program
        load,
when, what? — a clipper of the clouds popped up from leagues under
the verne sea, from earth to moon on twenty thousand spinning
        screws!
Neither prophet nor weird sisters helped me a whit, man nor woman,
nor sang the songs of travel; but unlocking the secret of the island
        code,
a captain without name encrypted it to the master of the world;
then, oh, this ramification of manual conundrums made me, like you,
        lose
command of the wordwand, and endure the entry-level pandora of
the sorcerer's apprentice who prized open the forbidden can of iron
        discipline!

A spiderman cadet sky-high on a network of girders,
I lacked, oh, a Tutorial or a TeachText or a Read Me
      First,
but down in the foreman's office sat widowed warlocks
chained to their zodiac terminals inputting digits from open
      folders —
when? — in the next millennium, and I felt like a weeping old-world
electrician dying to shortcircuit their wired webs of micro
      files.
For the way then they failed to heed me has given me ever since
a sense of not quite belonging to whatever world I move in, like the
      cursed
and wandering Jew forbidden to die; and it seems now that
wherever I go I'm mocked at by a kind of resignation in people's
      smiles,
or made to feel like a fullblown galleon at sea in the midst of Gaza,
magritted round with blackeyed sunspots and floating grey-white
      boulders.
And since then too, to open doors to unfamiliar places has always
clutched me with a dread — that beyond there might be unbroken
      miles
of wild sandhills and distant sinbad surf — a glaring agoraphobia,
as if the old man of the sea with his wiry legs locked round my
      shoulders
forced me to peer down into a puddle of fresh rain and suddenly
flung me through it — high into the clouded sky of a world appallingly
      reversed!

Cascading menus, floating palettes, emoticons and hanging indents
munge my ability to navigate the thrashing bitstream: I utterly
      lack
the attributes to troubleshoot a head crash, and if the blinking
cursor were to freeze into a screen burn-in, I know that the only
      way
out is to abort and restart; but dumb terminals – I'm one! –
cannot spool the shifting paradigms from their dithering grayscale
      caves.
I remember once when standing on a windy shore in Wales,
a child in the marram dunes watching the breakers one by one
      crack
down on the white wakes of their forbears, my mother told me I could
go and play on the beach when the tide went out; so I waited for the
      waves
to turn round and run retro away from the shore, and when
they never did that, blamed the seagods for letting nature run
      astray,
not knowing that the process of kerning the characters of a seascape
contains a hidden algorithm, though wiser now my erlking mind
      raves
rather at its own shortcomings – as if at this time I'm standing still,
still eye-beaming the sea as I stood then, adamant on that windblown
      day
that what I was waiting for to happen *would* happen, yet knowing,
and not being willing to admit, that the waves will not, ever, turn
      back.

And yet I am driven onward, dragging behind me the active
matrix of my headstrong intractability, and if I were to
    swear
that the moon was a white elephant, I could
prove that I was both right and wrong, and never need to
    admit
to an error of judgement – and why not? Because I believe it is
perfectly possible to accept that a black crow can also be perfectly
    white.
I once swore to a friend that the majority of mankind are happy,
and know now that his scorn then was justified, but could scarcely
    bear
to feel the heat of his cold stare when telling him I've since discovered
there's hardly an axon of real happiness anywhere and he was
    right;
for it's true – that the moment a man imagines perhaps he has
found paradise, that very thought itself foretells the end of
    it.
I think I am not alone in this frowardness; I believe now
that the greatest enemy a man ever has to
    fight
is his own self; and for any man to attempt to assert
he's a better man than another is is no better than to
    spit
into the wind; yet the feedback of this is that, if I seek
the Word of God any place other than in my own mind, it won't be
    there.

To set up the first page in the new manual of seamanship, therefore, *Urgh*
I must first open wide the modem portals of my own barkbound
    heart;
attempt to be honest, swear that a crow is black only (but it isn't!
it is blue also), be patient at what perchance I find in the grey
    catacombs
of my brain, and know how to analyze what others have
stuffed willy-nilly into it, and delete what's false from what is
    true.
Not to become lost in the labyrinth of this titanic liner I cruise in,
it's needful I acquaint myself with the blueprint of every
    part
the shipwrights worked on. Only then can I print-preview
the paged layout of the decks, and only then find out
    who
designed and who installed and who keeps shipshape,
if there is any sign of there being someone, each of the cabined
    rooms.
If not, I will never get wind of from any one of the portholes
whether the sea and the sky and the birds may all be
    blue
when the sun is shining; and, if not, the most splendidly
decked of the ship's saloons will soon come to resemble dark
    tombs,
by which to emerge from which unsubmarined and enlightened
there would also not otherwise be anywhere any kind of edifying
    art.

Open Sesame, then! How was the wizardry plugged in?
No matter how or how many times I input the Arabian
> charm,
the grey screen remains a closed wall, stoned like myself, and why?
Because – antique incantations, if they ever did, now wield no
> power;
or maybe there's insufficient charisma in my issued commands,
or I lack conviction – that if I will a thing so to be done it will *be*
> done.
Perhaps there is something in me of King Canute, whom
the waves denied, indifferent to his futile voice and raised
> arm;
or of Ethelred the Unready praying to God – for a victory
not granted since the battlefield of his faith had already been
> overrun.
It is easier perhaps, or perhaps not, to give up and gabble
a quick brown fox jumps over the lazy dog to say the aesop grapes are
> sour.
What I thought I needed to open up the rock is a magic lamp,
even an old one, that I can rub to conjure up a torus
> apparition;
but the only way to succeed in besieging a fortress is first to decrypt
the land's layout, the length of battlements and the height of every
> tower;
and above all, I know now, never to be angry or prone to impulse.
For, to win, in any onslaught, the mind must be, oh, most perfectly
> calm.

Yet, how to be calm when I'm never able to break loose
from the unsound ululations of the fretting ocean? Yes, even
      here,
in this hill-ringed valley far inland, there is no way to evade
that sighing, those murmured reiterations, even at those
      times
when there's perfect silence everywhere about me. A constant
tinnitus, which is not alone the sea's mania, but keens, and
      becomes,
without my knowing how, as glorious as the soaring chorales of all
angels and of all audible voices heard afar off yet always hovering
      near.
And sometimes, oh, it roars for hours on end, more boisterous
than the sea itself should I be beholding it; and sometimes it
      hums
like the wires of pylons strung regal across the moorlands, or like an
organist lying dead asprawl his live keyboards, or the held
      chimes
of a million bells that toll still in the ringing aisles of my brain.
Aye, perpetually there, a tuneless diesel-boom of rolled
      drums,
an air of crying children, the fluting of blue-plumed nightingales,
a skreigh that drills mile-deep down into Morar's black chasms, or
      climbs
skirling and golden up through the thundering sunblaze; and will
never leave me – as if my soul itself has become an eternally open
      ear.

And how not ever to be angry, when neither God nor man
has ever done enough to erase the chaos and open a new
> page
in the world's volume? Utterly to unclutter the confused,
the cross-wired, the fused gridlock of knowledge, to
> delete,
oh, all that's inessential – the debris of shattered dreams,
the sawdust of Nazareth, the embers of Europe; for if you once
> look,
you'll see that we stumble forever through petrified forests
and backwoods of catchpenny kickshaws, and I'm racked with this
> rage
that not enough has been done, or that no one has gusto or grok enough
or even the guts to – oh! – harrow the gone-to-seed garden that God
> forsook,
or to blast the dust from the shelves, to vacuum out the anchored
wordships from their white moorings, and begin again with a clean
> sheet.
It would be, oh, I am certain, so simple, only to blue-pencil through
all that has ever been written and open thereafter an unlettered
> book,
and then with infinitesimal care to inscribe it with such cannily
crafted words and those in a hand that's so perfectly
> neat,
that in one sentence only, or a single word, I could easily compile
anew a manual that would guide us, untrammelled, to a new
> age.

But who in the world will dare to do this, if the doing were
desirable? And now that decisions are needed, who can
>	decide?
I, yes, I have sometimes dreamed that I'm installed
the ultimate mogul sanctioned by God to sceptre indomitable
>	power,
the dominant driver in the vanguard of the non-linear
galactic caravan, not in any way attached to that whispering
>	clique –
the clans of the world's leaders; for not one thing concerns them
further than to hold fast to the reins and the arms of their throned
>	pride,
and so they've lost, as eros has, whatever they had of charisma.
But I'd be kindly as Christ was in the shopsoiled temple; I'd
>	wreak
havoc in heaven if I could get there; I'd be the steel-willed
captain of an iron-keeled ship whose daily decree it would be to
>	scour
the corroded decks and incinerate all symptoms of incipient
rust in the minds of the crew; oh, I'd be such a man who need
>	speak
but one word to command instant compliance. And I would land,
and scavenge the windswept palaces and arcades and in one
>	hour
clear them of their cowering inmates and scuttle the vermin,
leaving behind me, aye, I would, all the doors and windows open
>	wide.

Enter

Enter the seafarer, clad in the blue robes of my druid
grandfather, a harp in the crook of his left arm and his right
    hand
striking the chords of romantic exile, as he listens to the gulls
lamenting also, and wanders from land to land like an alias
    Celt,
a latterday Blondel searching and singing alien for his lost lord,
and at last hearing, from a liveware dungeon, the song's
    refrain.
A world when I was young I believed I lived in, where castles
were never in ruins, but glimmered alive with princes and maidens,
    and,
aye, such seafaring minstrels, who in the banquets that were
held nightly, renumbered enchanting tales of giants and dragons
    slain,
where mead-crazed warriors boasted of prowess in battle,
and young knights in glittering armour, and, oh, with shining eyes,
    knelt
down for favours from the ladies they loved; while out in the dark
among the cromlechs, grendels lurked across moors in the mists and
    rain.
It was so lovely to be warm indoors there, or, if not there in reality,
to dream that virtually it was so, and to believe in the dreams. I
    felt
I lived in a never-ending legend, a world braver, yet safer and more
enduring than the present, and longed, oh, never to leave that golden
    land.

And listen: I dreamed I was throned high up in the carved-oak
organ-loft of a gothic cathedral packed with a spellbound
> congregation,
the five manuals and flared pedals arrayed before me,
and thereupon struck in full crescendo one magnificent
> chord
and held it, then charged into another, and a third after,
and so built a resounding chorale that cyberfired the shuddering
> air
with the high resolution of my obedient limbs, so that
never before or since then had anyone heard so profound an
> improvisation;
and I dreamed then that such was my genius at the keyboards
that the whole world had heard of it and astounded wept
> there,
and the nine thousand pipes of the organ gleamed like the staggered
towers of a steel castle, above which the paeans, oh! hosannas of angels,
> soared
beyond heaven. And the dream swerved to where robed on the white
stones of an Olympian arena I declaimed lines from the world's most
> rare
cothurnian archives; where I rebound Prometheus, unblinded Tiresias,
outlorded Tamburlaine, and adieued the embarking Prospero;
> roared
more stentorian than their wars or tempests and no sound more
overwhelming save upon ending the ocean tumult of an unsurpassed
> ovation.

And suppose then I'd been given Ariel to play with, what would I
want to do with him without knowing if he were feminine or
    male?
Would I love him as Prospero did, or would I have wanted him mine,
harmonious charmingly, as Miranda was, wooed and won by
    Ferdinand?
Or would I curse as Caliban did, deprived of the maestro's daughter,
or wish Ariel a monarch from across seas not to love but rather to
    respect?
There's not a man among us who is not in part a woman,
and not a child who does not long to be a man; and not a
    tale
that has not elements in it of Ovid's Metamorphoses,
where Chaos evolves into concord in the cosmos, and the
    elect
gods turn into men, or as Narcissus did into flowers; and as in
the Midas myth, a thing will change if I merely touch it with my
    hand.
So that if today I were to toss a round pebble into the sea,
I will have transformed the entire universe forever and forever
    wrecked
whatever order it might have possessed until that moment;
which serves to prove that a single grain of seachange
    sand
contains as great a power, evil or good, as Prospero had
when he raised the tempest at the first sight of Alonso's dissonant
    sail.

We scarcely know what miracles or devastations lie within
our fingertips: so much that we do or is done is done by sheer
    chance.
A murderer might otherwise have become a saint; and if Ariel
really *were* mine, I might well take him warm into my
    arms
and kiss him as dearly as Paris kissed the lips of that blessed face
that launched a thousand ships, or, willy-nilly so, perhaps I would
    not.
A man who, loveless, has walked lonely for forty years
might one day, as I did, find paradise hiding in an unexpected
    glance;
or a man bereaved may lie down weeping in a garden
and dream of, across a stream, his precious pearl without a
    spot;
and if Absalom hadn't died, perhaps David his father might
not now be renowned as a giant-killer or famed for his fervent
    psalms,
nor Jesus of Nazareth proclaimed the promised Messiah.
The history of the world, however, is not alone of its leaders: it is
    what
you or I may do or say or stumble upon at any moment.
So, aye, it is greatly needful that we be aware of the possible
    harms
or blessings that float like ghouls or angels around us,
and prepared always for the joltings or the joys of random
    happenstance.

Yet it is often what we do not or cannot do that
makes us heroes; and I might have long since died of perhaps
    AIDS,
had it not been for the joy of knowing one June morning that
my longhand brainchild, an epic poem on Christ, had won
    recognition;
a triumph that that same afternoon took away the need,
though also uninhibited the nodding possibility, to
    destroy
the virginity of a manchild, a chorister, who came to my room
and sang me some of those same psalms of David: griefs and
    accolades,
and an anthem, too, that I'd heard him sing in chapel,
with a title so fitting – "This Have I Done for my True Love". My
    joy,
my love, my love of the sound his voice, my true love of
him, banished me and him from the system crash of churning
    perdition,
unchristian from the slough of despond – though before that
there'd often been days of giant despair, for he was, oh, such a
    boy
I would have died for, and nearly did die. No – because of a certain
concatenation of events, it was my destiny then not to bring to
    fruition
that hanging apple of the eye, and, aye, if it had been more than
a single kiss, I'd now be wandering lost forever in those deviant
    glades.

And yet if I *had* been ever able to enter, to take the primrose
path of that everlasting saturnalia, I cannot, for the life of me,
      say
what nature of jamboree bonfires I would there conflagrate.
I'm like Hadrian, who built a wall, yes, round himself, before he
      met
the lovely Antinoüs; or like Malatesta the machiavel when
interfaced with objects whose beauty moved him – rendered
      mute.
I'm like a child watching a bacchanal and never desiring
to join the sodom karaoke on that or any other carnivore
      day;
or like a young faun, oh, so much enamoured of the music,
yet never heeding the wild piping of Pan's
      flute.
And if I ever *were* to be called there I'd have to be totally
reschooled in a thousand new arts and quite unlearn the ethic
      alphabet.
I may be harlequined a crass fool for shunning the elysian cruise,
for thus denying what most of us would whoopee for; but the real
      root,
the true ginseng of my strength is that I believe that love, or, yes, lust,
unattained, leads to a yen, oh, a yin or a yang of love more ascendant;
      yet
a love which cannot be named, which, yes, though it might be
akin to it in intention, cannot ever wear a gimcrack badge like
      gay.

Then Ariel to me could never be as Miranda would,
nor ever I Miranda to him. No, rather it would
      be
that in him I recognized an icon, an image of myself
as I once was or, if not that I was, would
      dream
once to have been, and the longing then would
be simply to *become* him, to act his role in place of him, and
      then
to be loved for what I would then be as him; and, oh,
the envy of not having that burns so intensely in
      me
I can hardly bear it, as if all the days of my childhood
were a time wildernessed. And if I could, I would live
      again
myself Ariel; as if a rivulet, having rushed down and entered
the sea, wished once more to start up at the head of the
      stream!
And there have been times, yes, with a living Ariel I know now
– oh, and I have told him, and he understands this –
      when,
yes, we have walked together openly hand in hand,
and I've then thought that this and nothing beyond it is in itself
      supreme
heaven, a most perfect *friendliness* of loving, that needs never
to be augmented, being already, oh, the one epitome of peerless
      ecstasy!

And Miranda then, what would she be to me if *she* were mine?
Why, one in a garden of eidolons that might perhaps have winged
    higher
than Ariel – a jewel from the south of France, oh, my first such
doting upon maiden, held so golden a rose, till, one day, she simply
    went
away and married – oh, the irony of it! – a man called Jesus.
And once in Leningrad in the gilded foyer of a vast hotel, beneath the
    chandeliers,
a fleeting glimpse of one, I'm certain an exiled princess, whose
ondine eyes, caught once, instilled in me – still so! – oh, such unfulfilled
    desire.
Here, too, in the orient, are some remembered – one with so
enchanting a smile, and, oh, Hiroyo! – your irresistibly touchable
    ears!
But above all there is one here, here unnamed, my wedded
wife of twenty years, of whom I say that if angels were ever
    meant
to walk on earth, she is one of them. And looking back upon
this donna hinterland, I could here unveil my teens of cherished
    souvenirs
of such walking feminine wonders, some far older than I was
– a nanny who died at work quietly in the kitchen; a mother who
    spent
the long nocturnals hammering out her clavier sarabandes; or a
Thespian dame, whose memory, at ninety-four, burned still with crystal
    fire.

Memory – sometimes, true, my memory runs low and I must close
windows; but then come the times when I look forward and
    seek
to re-enter virginal dominions; for I've striven long, have racked
the remotest regimes of my mind to find, or to invent, just one
    word
that will render exponent the ineffable radiance of
what I believe to be true love; a tenderness I know always will
    sever
itself from the senses; a perpetual flash which is not remotely
libidin; which could allow me without distinction to kiss the
    cheek,
yes, and the lips, of an old man, madonna or boy; which fills me with,
with whomever it is I'm in love with, a happiness so perfect it
    never
would assail the realms of innocence; a word which, if it could be
chanted, must surely lie somewhere along in the song of the blue
    bird.
A new entry is now needed in every lexicon of the cosmos;
but I wonder, as I stand here overwhelmed by wonder, whether
    ever
I will find it – that word to express that kind of love I speak of,
that has not yet ever been spoken, and that no man yet has ever
    heard,
and yet, if I could learn it, that I would utter once only, and thereafter
never again enter any arena of the world, or desire therein to
    speak.

Edit

And then, after the dream, comes the waking, those times
when, knuckling the sleep from my eyes, I find myself
>hexed
by the apparition of a face unmasked in the morning glass,
and can almost see the white creeping up into my hair; when all the
>glamour
of last night's command parade is compressed into a knot of pain
behind my eyes, and the world and my tongue are waterless and
>grey.
And from this lowest common multiple of melancholia,
I pick up the remnants of the triumphal, and make plans for the
>next,
disheartened by having fathomed that what follows will,
no, never bring back the glories that are past; for there is no
>way
for me to stand up again and redeliver my magnificent orations;
well, I may try, but will knee-knocking fail to do more than foolishly
>stammer.
I may, yes, have indelible memories of keyboard genius, may
still charge on extempore; but I know, too, that whatever I now
>assay
will be little more than a child's whimper, for the ringing tones
of my gone grandiloquence are crushed into whispers by the
>hammer
that murders romance; for, no matter how splendid my renderings
may have been, the words have blacked out, and I must edit the
>text.

Thus, one day still tossed in the undressed salad of my green
days, to be told it was merely a processed play on an amateur
      stage,
a children's charade; and to find myself standing on the bare
boards unfloodlit, among the visible mechanics of a ruined
      masque,
and the whole illusion shattered by a door-slamming father,
a corybantine mother, and a crew of taunting brothers, and no
      applause.
But a good sword, aye, forged from hammered steel, can only be
strong if the metal can retain its memories of a former
      age,
but far more than that, can understand the true
meanings of the hammer's blows when the furnace
      roars,
and can endure them; and most of all, can be reconciled to
the murderous end that rings loud within the ironsmith's
      task.
There is no making of a man without anvils, and behind
the scintillant radiance of genius there's always a mordant
      cause.
Mountains can boast no beauty without volcanoes or glaciers;
it takes the searing of sand to hone the perfection of a Venetian
      flask;
and dreams are only induced to come true if first they've been
smashed, as a canary sings freedom only after having known the
      cage.

We act out a multitude of roles before we take off the masks
and learn then the look of the lines in our own
      faces.
The masks of teachers, doctors, lawyers, all of us – we wield fiction
to disguise fact, but, indeed, there *is* no fact without a former
      fiction.
Ajax was once perhaps a wanking boy, and Helen of Troy
an infant in soiled napkins; Einstein's relatively impossible
      dreams
roiled beyond the red star wars before he shifted them into science;
Columbus discovered the new world having first envisioned unknown
      places;
Michelangelo conceived David deep within the unchiselled stone;
and the angel anthems Amadeus heard – *they* inspired his requiem
      themes.
There is nothing armoured true, then, without a panoply of lies,
and not one law of cockerel logic without its spotted eggshell
      contradiction.
For what does it mean to be a man, when I myself have
minimal nipples without milk, and what is woman, manned with
      schemes,
as the Wife of Bath said, to wield power over men? And was it
only for John, the disciple he loved, that Christ endured his crucial
      affliction?
There is always another way of looking at those things we've always
known to be true, just as a closed fist is, if you look, packed with open
      spaces.

So the seafarer shrinks to a lowercase sailor, or something less,
and instead of the sea-blue druid robes he dons his bell-bottomed
    jeans,
and the castles are real ruins now or revamped as hollywood sets
for giggling tourists to goggle at; and the harped lays erode into
    pop
ditties souled out by stoned teenagers, whose sourdine blues
are trumped into red giants by the feedback hertz of wowing
    speakers.
And the battles fought now are with knives in the ganged streets;
and a favour bestowed on a knight leers in an eyed smile that
    means
your place or mine; and Tom Thumb and the seven-league boots
he strode in are yawning graders in trodden-down-at-the-heel
    sneakers;
and the monsters that prowl in the neon shadows are the winsome
narcotics peddled to the young, who have no knowhow how to
    stop
needling these Edens. And dragons, though still dreamt of,
are programmed down into animation quests, and little kids are the
    seekers.
The entire pageant of the romantic has gone past, and with soiled
greenbacks instead of gold, a valiant adventure can be bought in a
    shop;
and the gods of Parnassus, the grandeurs of Rome – what now
but knickerbocker glories we lick from the finger taps of our laptop
    machines?

A child of these times can wreak miracles faster than Christ,
can alice up wonderlands by a single button push or the pull of a
      lever;
no longer needs tutorial drills to make things with his hands, needs
only to joystick his hot-rod fingers to command and operate cold
      toys.
On a family motor-trip through the blue barbaric beauty of Scotland
will never once glance up from the minuscule screen of his bitmapped
      game.
Knows nothing or next to it of the satisfaction of a thing achieved
by brow sweat, has no inkling of the real industry of a dam-building
      beaver.
Has never scanned even the graphic images of his own imagination;
has lost his dynamic – a sabre-toothed tiger spoonfed and grown
      tame.
Has little sensation of setback, anticipates freeware rather than
adversity, not knowing that hardship's the only way to realize true
      joys.
And, yes, like my former self, cries out for playthings the same day
they're daydreamed of, even before they're anointed with number or
      name.
The little children have thus burgeoned into brutal despots in a world
where the adults backwater back again into mere girls and trepid
      boys.
And a child may warp and woof in the worldwide web of ergonomics
without ever having learned, or of, the craft of the croft-bound
      weaver.

Vision of our times?

It's an age of have now in a world where the have nots
outnumber the haves a thousand to one, or more likely
> more;

where virtue is little more than a misspelled version of vice;
where the pop-up heroes of the mainline young are skin-pop
> junkies;

where cocaine can change hands quicker than a can of Coca-Cola can;
where the grown grass, no longer green, goes up to heaven in
> smoke;

where any kind of bedfellow at any age is condoned; where kids
are trained in condom mechanics without knowing what they are
> for;

where conked-out love conquers all and ends up conquering itself;
where anything that smacks of decency is bullied as a sick
> joke;

where men and women, supposedly the high ends of evolution,
now ape the apes and screw ad lib like rabbits or gibbering
> monkeys;

where often, aye, the most saintly of leaders, or a pillar of state
standing erect, is revealed as a leaking phallus wrapped in a
> cloak;

where the jaggers and jacksons and madonnas are crowned queens,
and erstwhile kings assume the obsequious, oversexed roles of peruked
> flunkeys;

where liberty's a carcass monument riddled with human worms,
and justice is weighed in the carat scales of ingot
> law.

Yet, yes, there are compensations: we must not imagine
that everyway pathway leads downward; I must never
> think
that tomorrow I'll be a day older without some tangible
benefit or that white hair is a nimbus damnation; think of the
> eyes
and the things I can now do with them I'd never dreamed of:
the blessings of long sight, not literal merely but also their fractal
> metaphor.
The mountains of Cymru, take them, there are few older,
which, as the boy – still in me! – gazed at, would seem to
> shrink
far off and further into blue nebulance, but which now, if
at sixty-three I view from a certain sandhill on the Tremadog
> shore,
will halloo their miracles of detail; aye, to pick out the pinnacled
crags of the Glyders; to watch the smoke of the mountain train
> rise
high in the wind above the Saddleback; to see clearly the castle
at Criccieth across the bay – and so everywhere oh, so much
> more
lovely is everything I look at that was remotely beautiful
in the past. Yet here's the paradox: I might find the scanned
> skies
smirched with things more obviously ugly; but, if that were so,
it would never unbird for me the blue radiance of that dreamer
> Maeterlinck.

The blue bird, then, what is it? Why does it sometimes seem
as blue-black as the raven, or why a seagull grey-backed and off
    white?
Is it only the past that is constant, and the present and future
constantly restless? The sea, like the fishes within it, never lies
    still;
and all the rivers of the Earth run shining down into the sea,
which is never full, aye, never fulfilled, yet the ocean is still
    there.
And so it may be with mankind – that there is not any thing
we're anchored to that will not let go of us, or at any moment
    might.
The saddest bones of a man's skull are those that scurr his tragic
temples: bewilderment dwells there, as if the mind within is only half
    aware
of having left the primeval, and it seems equally possible that,
at the thule end of evolution, he'll likewise lose hold of his own
    will.
Just as he loomed like a phantom galleon from deluvian darkness,
so he will drift in his lost ark through the labyrinths of the cyberian
    thoroughfare.
No matter what, there is one thing certain that moves upward:
though the present is a wheel of words that spins like a mancha
    mill
running haywire, and though the past is a locked file we can read only,
the future is one we can, oh, that we *can*, at this point in time, still
    write.

But no matter what we've done with or made of the undone world,
or no matter how much we have clipped the wings of the blue
    bird,
it is better always to suffer the little children to come to us
and forbid them not, for of such is the kingdom, and the living
    young
are all we'll ever leave behind us to carry the scarred grail
up the aluminian gangway of the ship of the evolving future
    tense.
That is why the best thing a man can do is to take the best
paleoliths of the past and make them pearls of the future. *Lo! we have
    heard
of the glory of the kings of the people*, and surely we must re-tell
these tales to our children, yet keep them as long as we can in shining
    innocence;
for there are, yes, aristo ways of waking and walking to the window,
and of seeing the world as golden and not as a necklace of pearls
    unstrung,
trashed and scattered on the slagheaps of a black maria motherland.
We must therefore select the paramount jewels of our hoarded
    experience,
and find the most fitting fonts for the penmanship of the young
upon the purest of watermarks, so the songs they compose may be
    sung
all the more sweetly than we ever sang them, that their ships may sail
on the sea, oh, so much nearer than we could – to the perfect, uneditable
    Word.

III *Ship*

Save

Save the sea, what other source to save is there save
ourselves and the ships we sail in? And what can we
      do
towards this needful salvation? Or, more pertinent, what can
I do? If I were Noah and God-commanded I would
      rebuild
the ark and wait for the next deluge, but with God so seasick,
can I trust now in the promise of a rainbow, and would the
      dove
have wings buoyant enough to bear the olive branch,
bring it to the open window and fly away thereafter into the
      blue
firmament never to return? And I wonder now also whether
God still has the will or the willingness or enough
      love
of us to care for our survival, and whether there's any likelihood
whatever now of our resurrecting the shining hyperions we have
      killed.
It seems more than probable that the shuttling messengers
that lance the ozone will bring back to us from the good heavens
      above
a static cacophony of woof-words far worse than the first Babel,
and the most canny and alert of captains won't be remotely
      skilled
enough to unweave the outlandish lingoes of other welkins, or live
long enough to browbeat the time warps that cross-wind him and his
      crew.

We should never think, then, of launching another Nautilus,
made for a star trek twenty thousand light-leagues long, without
>understanding
what happened to the Challenger up and Columbia down, even if
their million-dollar rest rooms *were* the last word in paradise; or
>how
much nearer we are to the cavemen than to Dan Dare, and that
Stonehenge is hardly more primitive than a digitally mastered
>clone
of it. Observe how the Mach-two Concorde descends like a swan
ugly above water, and listen to the primal shriek of its deafening
>landing:
the searing touch of tyre and tarmac somehow seems now to antedate
the pluperfect conjugations of the Hammurabi Code or the Rosetta
>stone;
and the newest fangled and yet-unrevealed blueprints of the future
perfect seem more decrepit than the Dead Sea scrolls or the Golden
>Bough.
And yet – Volkswagen Beetles seem so quaintly human we chide them
for disasters on the autobahns when the fault has always been our
>own.
Because, though, of our affection for these folkcraft we've created,
we lovingly restore them, smithsonian them and proudly
>endow
them with mystical charismas. But – although thus we save them,
we must take heed that the files of the world's hardware are forever
>expanding.

And the more we go surfing tipsy through the topsy-turvy
wavelengths of the internet, the more our topsail skills become
      inferior;
and the more hours logged on-line inputting trash or downloading it,
the less retrievable will become the ability to output appassionata
      thunder.
There's no triumph in being an armchair journeyman or a net potato,
or in overloading couched brains till they leak from our stuffed
      ears.
For such is the frantic pandemania to save every atom of information,
that even the sanest of us stand now on the thresholds of world-wide
      hysteria.
It is not today far-fetched to imagine that when grief comes, perhaps
tomorrow, our eyes will run with virus ampersands instead of
      tears.
But, oh, what little gadfly among us has a voice bold enough
to challenge the spider and untangle the webs into which we all
      blunder?
Not one has courage to utter the obvious, aye, for fear of the mainline
scoffs of the wavetop trippers or the media-potheads' spoilsport
      jeers.
There are no lifeguards left on the beaches to cry out the alarm
as the data-crunching driftnets drag down the drifters, aye, down and
      under;
and I see the day when – when the cue pops up with a "Save Now?" –
the last man alive will cry "Save *me*!" and drown in the red tides of
      Cyberia.

Is it needful, then, to save our memories of journeys? Or is it alone
the vehicles and vessels that we voyage in that deserve our
    attention?
Or is it where they come from or where they go to, or what's seen
from the windows that's the essence of the nostalgia, and also
    who
is with us? After an odyssey overseas or a drive of five hundred miles,
my ears still drumming with the highway thunder, I've often wondered
    whether
such rovings were dreams, whether nothing's real to us save only these
dazed aftertimes of reminiscence. It seems to me now more than half
    invention
that one Wednesday twenty-five Augusts ago I was lost, yes,
inside the Kremlin, yet the Monday following found a kittiwake's stray
    feather
on my way, where? – over the sea to Skye. I've journals to prove this –
that I was there then, but can I believe them? *Was* I there? Was it
    true?
And what if I *were* there, is there any pith in it – to believe as Deor did
that *that has passed, and so may this* be a long past *song of us two*
    together?
Or that afternoon, rushing by rail across Poland with love from Russia,
in such a train, so clear the picture – the scent of pasture sweeping in
    through
the window, a pair of flash-past cantering ponies hitched to a haywain,
and the young driver cheerio waving – to talk of it now, is it worthy of
    mention?

Oh, save them! Forbid them to be forgotten, say, such memories
as this one: – Rolling north from Nakhodka hard-class on the long
      train
to Khabarovsk, the enormous woman in the sweltering kitchen
of the restaurant car, at a tiny stove – oh, the toil of it! – shovelling
      coal;
and Lilya the worn-out waitress, a harassed housewife, who,
when I begged her to give me a Russian-tea tumbler, just one, for a
      souvenir,
told me she didn't dare to, but then promised that if on the way back
I again asked her, yes, *then* she would – knowing that we'd never meet
      again.
But, eight weeks later – oh, Lilya! – there she was in the same diner!
And without a word, and with a smile not without a flicker of
      fear
in it, she handed me the glass in its tin-plated holder. Remembering
such little kindnesses as this kind nurtures, oh, the deepest benthos of my
      soul.
I am quite certain that each one of us has recollections akin to this,
which are not to be filed away and forgotten, but will affect us
      year
after year, teaching us how to live better in the now and the hereafter,
and are never, therefore, to be thought of as moribund, but play a vital
      role
in the making of mankind; and there's, no, not one incident of the past,
that, recalled and held precious thus, may not move us to become more
      humane.

There's a danger, though, that such maudlins of memory
may render us mere automatons of numskull
      retrospection,
depriving us of the faculty of looking forwards without weeping
at the mindstunning gridlock of the fractal future; so we'll become
      older,
even senile, in our adolescence, and enter our second childhood
long before the first is finished, and wallow in the fens of ambrose
      sentimentality.
We have to learn then how to select the text we will work with,
how to winnow grain from the chaff, and print that out – the final
      selection.
But how is it possible to do this? Every minute as I sit here I am
growing older and inching inexorably nearer to my life's
      finality,
and the duration of waiting for godot – as it grows palpably shorter,
so does the shot scenario lengthen, written and stored in memory's
      folder.
Going to school by train I'd always be sure to be facing the engine,
but now, in my sixties, I sit with my back to it: for this is the glaring
      reality –
that it's more heartwarming to look at the past, at the things that
might have been have-beens, at the neverlands too; and, oh, so much
      colder
to contemplate, not what happiness may come to me tomorrow,
but the notion that all that I now remember will one day be denied
      resurrection.

On the bookshelf above my desktop is the wooden clock
I learned to tell the time by when I was eight or perhaps
    nine.
But who will hear of this a hundred years onward, and is it mere
vanity to grieve that I might be gone from here with such a fact
    unknown?
Can I bear to think that the entire network of my thoughts,
every dream and all my memories, will one day simply cease to
    exist?
When a man dies, there is such irrecoverable loss of treasure,
as if having just tapped the optimum vein he must shut down the uncut
    mine.
It makes me wonder why I have to be here at all, why have to learn
anything, when all the brain's whispers will dissolve like a morning
    mist.
What is the wisdom in becoming wise, or of ever trying to achieve
any kind of end, when an end will come anyhow to all I can call my
    own?
That clock, handworked by a craftsman dead now – my grandfather
bought it, my father and aunt bickered over it – it's become a ticking
    catalyst,
an igniter of personal legend. But what of it? And yet, is there anything
anywhere more important than this? Or more than the shining grey
    stone
I picked up yesterday on the seashore? What has priority?
God or mankind? Christ or his disciples? The cast pearls or the cursed
    swine?

A pig has — hasn't it? — as much right to exist as the Pleiades,
and might have the power to render us here on Earth far greater
    pleasures
than the crackling stars; yet what do we do? — Laugh at the poor
animal, bacon it, serve it up roasted, sometimes the entire
    head.
Why should we imagine the pinhead patterns of the sky more
beautiful? We kill things without thinking, without sorrow, without
    caring,
identical to the way we're doing our best to slaughter the Earth;
and most likely we'd murder Orion if we took the proper
    measures
or had other means to achieve it. *Wouldn't* we? Surely, then,
oh, isn't this asinine indiscriminate assassination beyond
    bearing?
Yet galaxies collide and commit their own heavenly pogroms,
and the skies are filled with stars doomed to die, or dying or already
    dead.
To save which may mean to destroy much that might have been saved
by calculated destruction. Lemmings understand this and die without
    despairing,
somehow knowing that flowers flourish best in a weeded garden.
Might it not be better, then, to lay waste to kit and caboodle, and
    spread
the ashes evenly throughout the universe? For, how, when the hard
cores of all shining raindrops are motes of dust, can we call them living
    treasures?

Oh, but save the fireflies, for they are surely
delegates from heaven, bringing us most wonderful
      revelations —
that if we persist thus to abuse the sea and molest the sea's
children, we'll shut down forever the furnace of the human
      mind.
The fireflies, they appear here, in this green valley in the early summer,
and so tenderly hopeful hover glimmering over the dulcet unhurrying
      stream.
And it seems then, in the evenings, as if the very stars themselves
have come down with messages for us expressed in the gentle
      pulsations
of their airborne lamplights, oh, somehow to save their souls;
and it's so much as if we can see the stars' instinct, for they
      seem
to be, in and out, breathing in the darkness; and there was one
that came solitary to my window and hung there throbbing with a
      kind
of urgent asking for me to be willing, oh, to do something and do it
soon enough; and others of them rose high up into the night to
      gleam
in unison with the distant constellations, as if they wished to return
to heaven with glad tidings, which, if they could, would be for them to
      find
their mission completed; and would be also, in this tragic and ravaged
world we live in, the most miraculous and most heart-warming of all
      salvations.

Print

Ahoy, there! cries a crewman from the crow's nest across
the green-grey ongoing granite of the swaying ocean, but is not
    understood,
for there's no ship in eyeshot and no seafarer other than his
own shipmates, and the Earth's ocean is, most certain, uniquely
    alone
in the cosmos. Our solitary hull needs a captain who knows well
how to sail it and above all who loves, aye, idolizes the crying and stoic
    sea!
A lifeboat, designed to sail forwards, can, if so commanded,
grind backwards through the water, though, if left to the wind,
    would
go the way of the weather; and this is surely the best – to have
at all times sound fellowship with the elements. For, to remain
    free
of the miseries of seasickness, one must be perfectly at one with
the rising and falling of the ship's keel, and the sea's whims
    foreknown.
And out of these soundings – that there is nothing but upbeat
headwork in the planned piloting of a voyage from outset to its
    apogee –
I may thus format a principle – and, oh, I believe in it! – that will
render an answer to the human conundrum and leave not one
    stone
unturned. And that credo is simply this: that there does exist,
intangibly here and elsewhere, but incontrovertibly, one unconditional
    good.

They don't

A tree always grows and is, till the moment of its death,
still growing. It never, I am sure of it, endeavours to
>   die.
Growing has resolve in it, dying is not deliberate.
Here, then – at last! – is an article of seamanship I can
>   take
as a manifesto to live by. Ah, but the lemmings, you'll ask me,
why do they leap into the sea? Why, surely, only that others may
>   survive
after them. But isn't there a darkness here, in this beam of luminance?
Though the shadow of a tree revives a parched Saracen, it may also
>   deny
sunshine to flora or fauna that cannot live without the sun.
Yet there's surely something upward and ongoing in this perpetual
>   drive
to remain living as long as possible; for a wave on the shore
condones suicide only to make seaway for the next breaker in its laced
>   wake.
To set the ripples ringing wider – if everything that ever has being
has to die also, then everything not yet given the gift to be
>   alive
will be given that; which is to say, that whatever things we may
today think of or imagine that are not here yet will, like buds,
>   break
open into flower in the sunshine, and become miracles we have
ourselves created. Am I God then? Now there's a reason to wonder
>   why!

Why not? If I can dream of anything I want to and believe it
can indeed become reality, I really can build castles in the
    air!
And if I'm nostalgic for a god I can talk to, I can genie one
into existence, and it's quite possible he'd be an absent-minded old
    man
with a white beard, with twinkling and kindly eyes, who would
always forgive me, if so I chose it. It so happened that when
    young
I was a sworn atheist, but as I grow nearer now to annihilation
I am so overwhelmed with the wonder of and love of the
    rare
miracle of being here that I cannot deny a divinity framed it;
and it comes to me clearly that the long-gone sages have already
    sung
the long anthems of it and fervently I listen to them still sounding –
in the still disciplines of Zen, say, or in the frescoed marvels of the
    Vatican.
So Wordsworth came to deem Nature less worthy than God's Word,
and the Waste Land finder found a quiet homeland and a holy
    tongue
to verse in as an Anglican verger. It matters not what names
I give to the gods I worship, for all are components of the teetotal
    plan,
symbols of the awe I am heir to; nor need I look for an apodixis,
for inscrutable telekineses abound, and within them – the answers are
    there!

Even if a bamboo tree one day puts forth a swansinging
flower to denote or annotate the decease of an entire
      grove
of them, that flower's a harbinger, a messenger of good cheer,
a promise of progeny, and, I reiterate it, I do absolutely
      believe
there is unconditional goodness always about us,
no matter what boo-birds caw-caw that faith as a gaga
      fiction.
This, then, is the glistening aura of the overall ocean,
the way I will look upon my every ship, and every island,
      cove
and promontory, and every mountain, city and spire, the haloes
I'll believe my crew companions have – all blessed with this golden
      benediction,
and even, too, the very seawinds that fulfill my sails.
And if I know this and never lose it, I know then I will never
      grieve
further as long as I live – for every sorrow will be turned
somehow into happiness, and every birdcage of human
      restriction
become a kind of findhorn freedom. And no matter how surely
I'm one day condemned to die, there's a – oh, yes there is! – a shining
      reprieve
in knowing that the death of the god in me will kindle a new one,
just as Christ was a phoenix that rose from the ashes of Olympian
      Jove.

And if Jehovah, once so jealous, became gentle by Christ's intervention,
then like John I may write the things I have seen, for it is
      man
that christens the deities and not they who create man, though
somehow mankind has come here – from the forces that burn in and
      burn
out the stars. I have, and so do any of us have, a perfect freedom
to set up the godhead we think we will love and will love us
      best.
And perhaps mine will be a kind Adonis, but without Venus
to seduce him, or Ganymede without Jupiter; a white-haired Peter
      Pan
imbued with the bright-eyed wisdom of Homer, who sits on a hillside
and sings arcadians to his listening lambs. And he will be
      blessed
with a maiden companion perhaps a little like Marina of Mitylene;
and with forget-me-nots for prayer books they will lovingly together
      learn
the virtues of matrimony, and bring into the world then children
who will walk silvern like Ariel siblings, and discover the filigree
      nest
the blue bird has built golden in a willow tree above them.
And this will remain the renewed Eden whose denizens will never
      yearn
for a lovelier paradise – where a harp of Burma is heard somewhere
beyond Samarkand and nearer to the welkin perhaps than a land like
      Bhutan.

And there would be warm springs there mezzo-limonading up
under and through the waters of a lake so perfectly
> pure
that a snowflake would be visible nineteen fathoms down,
where the world's leaders would assemble, unclad – an open
> convention
where all conventions are outcast, and protocol closed down,
where kings and presidents, empresses and imams will
> repose
together in a kind of rose-garden harmony hitherto unknown,
aye, snicker if you will. And the health-bringing waters will be a
> cure
more certain than any yet concocted for the ills of this war-wracked
world. And attendants will come jocund there and gently
> enclose
them in cool garments that bear no emblem of nation or standing;
and jingo olympics will be banned, or, if held, held naked and with no
> intention
other than to demonstrate the common humanity of the world's people,
no matter where they may hail from. Oh, pooh-pooh on! Not one of us
> knows
a way better to eradicate the heartburn of the human predicament!
Not one of us has nerve or magnanimity enough to dream of a total
> suspension
of pessimism, nor dares to encode an evangelist declaration,
a communiqué not for that event only, but one, such as this, that will
> endure:

I have learned how to love a thing as a leaning to be given only
and demanding nothing. I have learned that virginity is a
    pearl
not to be thrown to the swine, and is not, as a pearl is,
an unwanted beauty it cannot abstain from
    creating.
Learned how to judge and be gentle at it,
how to smile at contempt. Learned to enjoy life without
    killing
the joys radiant within it. Learned the seasons,
that dusk is a widdershins dawn, that a flower will always
    unfurl
from a bud if left to do so, and, yes, that there may be trials
and errors of wormwood in the workings of nature, though not
    willing
ones. I have learned how to be never-endingly thankful
for having been given this day the living daylight, and never to be
    waiting
for the sanguine handsels of tomorrow, when there is always
delight to be found in every moment, if I remember how
    thrilling
it is simply to be alive, aye, even in the catacombs of sorrow.
Learned that merely thinking that I can do *this* is forever
    germinating
a thought of doing *that* – the seed of greater endeavour; that the boy
grows stronger in the man, and in each crone remains always the lovely
    girl.

I have learned also that whatever is tiny is also a titan,
who must learn, too, how to love being a pigmy. Learned that a
      slice
or two of new bread with cheese and a fresh tomato will do as well
as the most sumptuous of banquets, which are themselves not things to
      shun
whenever they're spread before me. Learned that every heartbeat
is one of a possible three billion, and meeting my childhood
      friend
after an age apart of fifty years, learned that the friend's heart,
and mine too, has been beating all that while – and that
      paradise
is little more than simply knowing a thing like that, and thinking
of it as a miracle of human endurance. Learned, too, that the far
      end
coming to a thing is near the beginning of another, which has,
before the ending of that which precedes it, already
      begun.
I have learned that if the human body is akin to a landrover,
the brain might be likened to the driver of it, and to
      spend
a lifetime tuning engines or touching up paintwork, will avail nothing
– unless also I keep my mind's binnacle as bright as the morning
      sun.
For if the car of Phoebus Apollo, or any system within that, crashes
when driven amiss, the same goes for every other man-engineered
      device.

Likewise all ships, and the men who made and man them, and the sea
they sail in – are not without limit, for even a simple wooden
      splint
derives life from the death of a tree that might otherwise have been
the fuel to drive the starlight express, which itself will one day be
      consigned
random to the scrapyard and melted down into – perhaps a nail,
which might then cause human lifeblood to scar crimson the dying
      ocean.
This is the fiery frozen concatenation of all things and time
in the cyber dimensions reduces all sense of voyaging to the merest
      hint
of being here or going elsewhere, creating a motionless wormball
as gaudy as the excrement of a zoo monkey. Yet I know there will be
      motion
in my own dimension, a journey I am now making, and upon which
I may visit all the sun-blessed islands of my dreams, a journey
      defined
in heaven and which will end there, no matter how many hells I may
encounter, for I know now how to confront them, and how by pure
      devotion
to goodness to be free of tribulation, though I may weep sometimes
when sorrow comes. And if I myself know this, and if it is known to all
      mankind
that there is unconditional good inherent in every article of seamanship,
it will be possible to declare here indelible beatitude in this, the final
      print.

Shut Down

It rushes in so suddenly, this wisdom — *is* it wisdom? — that one day
I'll have to die, that the long open application has to be shut
      down.
And on the way there, limping through the overloaded fly-blown
greenaway sets of this million-mullioned stageboat in which I've been
      sailing,
I see the candles one by one sputtering out, lanterns of the living,
those that have led me or looked askance at me, but have moved
      on
before me. Yet it seems while learning there's nothing constant, no,
not in the dust of Alexander, nor in the skulls dug up by the graveyard
      clown,
that we never learn till it's too late that we ourselves are destined
to be a part of that transience; nor are we ever really ready to be
      gone
away from here or prepared to be snuffed out — unless we are men
who love kevorkian endings when our will to linger longer is
      failing.
As for myself, let it be where I can gaze upon the evening sun
sinking behind the sea, as gentle and as beautiful as a dulcitone
      chaconne,
with the long yarning surf as a slow passacaglia, and let my ashes drift
down from the fanged crags of Crib Goch and join the alleluia
      wailing
of gulls in the mist-cloaked air of old Snowdonia, and if I could choose
my way of leaving, in a mandala of seadreams let me unknowingly
      drown.

Aye, for the sea is calling me always. For years, on vacation, I've plied
the black currents from Boso to Tosa in a derelict Nippon
      ferryboat;
and at night sometimes, leaning alone on the rusted white railings,
have felt, oh, this irresistible pull from the dark gleaming waters to
      leap
down into them, and I think I would do that, were it not that I cannot
sustain the thought of my truelove, aspen-tender, asleep in our cabin
      below,
standing next morning forlorn on the car-deck by our ivory-white
Nissan van, having scoured the ship for me, for a farewell
      note
or for some sign for her why I had done that. Perhaps it is true –
I've often thought this – that the most cruel among us, I being one,
      show
more sentimentality than others kinder do. For – what *is* this?
Why does the dismal seem so delicious – to make one so close to me
      weep
thus? And why is it that whenever we descry any stretch of water,
we're so excited by it, cry out and point, and like me, wish to
      throw
ourselves headlong into – or is it *back* into? – is it our mother's womb?
There's something wanting, something wanted in there, in the deep, too
      deep
for me to comprehend; yet I hear that voice forever calling me,
as if the ocean's ancient matriarch, dying long, desires a lifelong
      antidote.

Isn't there perhaps a longing in all of us for a like panacea,
and if we cannot find one, a desire then, oh, for a blessed
     release?
Our ships, our cities, our mechanizations have grown so far beyond
gargantuan we cannot manage them, and we live like buzzing
     flies
with brains that never sleep; have become too cerebral ever again
to be heroic the ways Odysseus was; and there's nothing more to
     explore
save inaccessible stars. And the space between what we are now,
a race at the point of extinction, and finding life elsewhere or a golden
     fleece
hanging somewhere in the heavens – is too great ever to be spanned.
And to be original, unique, to be hip and with it always, becomes the
     more
unattainable the more we flounder in the morass of what's now called
civilization – a world cynical, a world two-faced, a world of smiling
     lies.
And those of us who win fame in it – are we happy ever? Not truly,
for the kinds of criterion we measure happiness by are decayed to the
     core,
and we bask in our tabloid renowns, and never again may enjoy
solitude as a man unknown can, who can hear our despairing
     cries –
the elvis cataclysms, the hendrix jeremiahs – only for the next coming,
not Christ's reincarnation but the carnal kind – creaming kairos without
     surcease.

Less than half awake at the best of times, and in half-darkness always,
I interface the living world as through a body-bag of misted
    polythene.
All sounds to me have never seemed analog, but somehow
hidden in a veil such as when music comes digital to me, not wholly
    here
in this room I listen in. As if I am still far nearer to being almost
all animal than anything all-knowing as we dream of God as
    being.
I watch my finger draw patterns on the moisture of a window
pane, but the hand doing that seems an avatar's other than mine,
    seen
as a handycam might catch it, a kodak brain that has no faculty
to understand what it is doing, and as if what it is
    seeing
is also nothing more than an image of reality; as if all is always
virtual, all otherwhere, and nothing anywhere here perfectly
    clear.
And even if the origins of the universe ever become known to us,
will we ever know what it is there for? Will wisdom always be
    fleeing
beyond what we think of when we think we know everything?
There are still times, so tantalus-ridden, when, oh, I am so
    near
to grasping it, but find, after reaching out with my hand
to touch it, that all I can feel is the warm glass of an unbreakable
    screen.

Here at my keyboard I'm little more than a mere letter-linker.
And if you were to ask me how *exactly* these bitmap inputs are
      processed
in the innards of the windowed whirligig I work at, how it
stomachs what I feed it with, I would find it utterly beyond me to
      expound.
Someone, no doubt, could blueprint its brainwaves for us, but that
wouldn't bible the miracle of computation nor make me a better
      poet.
Perhaps that's how it is with God and man – that God gives us
the ships to sail in and then abandons them, leaves us to do our
      best
to master the seacraft and the crafts of the sea without ever knowing
what alien port we are bound for, and gives us no means to
      know it.
Or it may be, to mirror this, that God is a man-made machine,
which, if I took trouble enough I could dismantle from the
      ground
up and analyse down to the last bit – to find out how God
works, but such an undertaking would so daunt me I would
      blow it,
or blow it up and blow away the wonder of not knowing. For –
not knowing is perhaps a better a way of finding the never to be
      found
bird that's blue as the sky, which, aye, I do see as delectably blue,
but, if I look deeper, might find is as black as annihilation and totally
      unblessed.

What Homer was, who knows it? But a voice after him has come
down to us in the voices of others, into and out of miraculous
      holes
in the lanternine skulls of those who heard them and learned later
how to record them by hand — aye, the human hand that has
      made
all that is not seaborn or earthling. Then struck the caxton wavecrest
breaking in with renaissant print-outs, and knowledge began to
      freeze,
growing like an iceberg abscess under the ocean, till mankind was
so keyed up he was, what? — Shipwrecked on the remington
      sholes,
which themselves did not preclude voyaging, but rather hastened it
onward to the terminal selectric inventions of our own era. It is
      these,
more than any other, that have thrust us on to the next,
the newest tideline of evolution, where man, the flesh of him, is
      overlaid
with a metallic skin, within which he struggles like the half-blind
nucleus of an amoeba, multiplying cells through the prison walls he
      sees
on every side of him. The computer is not the last of our ships,
for we will sail beyond it into a gigabyte world we'll seek to
      upgrade
forever, but while doing so, will assassinate our humanity,
and herald the end of what we have hitherto known as human
      souls.

And yet we are here still, little thinking creatures
strutting like half-fledged chanticleers and picking over every
      stone
in the cluttered farmyard, looking for our partlet chicks. We are still
so endearingly old-fashioned in our coxcomb fashions and bumbling
      modes
of living; and perhaps it is here that we may find salvation;
for to become doddering gardeners growing dahlias or string
      beans,
or to perch on deckchairs in the sunshine with our cups of tea,
or idly to hum – *Knick-knack, paddy-whack, give a dog a*
      bone,
This old man comes rolling home – or to lounge in our favourite
armchairs in front of the TV or to browse through glossy
      magazines,
or to go surfing for the fun of sunburn; to sit in the pub
talking of old times, or to take long walks along green country
      roads –
are things we enjoy more and seem at loggerheads with the hideous
apparition of the alternative – cold technology on the rocks. This
      means
we must hold on forever to the manual of ships we know how
to handle, before we commit or condemn ourselves to break the
      codes
of the unknown future. And we must remember, and it is so sad to, that
no matter how many bright faces are about us, man is irrevocably
      alone.

And I am one among such men, standing alone now on the shore,
hearing the keening or the wistful voices in the waves, and
      knowing
so well now what they are saying, and I am so doldrum-dashed
that so few of us are tutored to listen. And I see the shining
      eyes
of the young, and I am, oh, so sorrow-sick to think what they
will have to contend with. Perhaps, though, I do not need to
      gaze
so far into the future as I'm gazing, or no further into the past.
We rarely know of or think about the frayed or frail lifelines
      flowing
beyond our grandfather's father or our son's grandson;
we merely cling to the rigging of our ship through the stormy
      days,
or stand local in the prow or astern awhile, and see only
white horses a little way ahead or a solitary gull in the wake that
      cries
following us, for perhaps companionship a little; and that one
seabird, without angst or anguish, can choose a thousand
      ways
to wing elsewhere, and does willy so or nilly does not and mews
in the wind without knowing either joy or grief, until the day it
      dies.
Let us take, then, that gull as an emblem for us, and seek to be
living always, without caring neither what life is nor where we are
      going.

I'll never know, perhaps, who assigned this, or whether the task is
yet accomplished; nor if there exists here or anywhere an infallible
    art
of seamanship compiled, or to be so, for everyman or myself only.
It may be my ways of wondering have been too random, too
    undisciplined
to render coherent meaning to this manual I set my hand to.
And what shall I say to the wayward, and how shall I let them
    know?
I'd like them to shun the carefree arts of destruction they excel in,
to find joy in the making of things that give joy to others – before they
    depart
with nothing done save the undoing of themselves. Those who *know*
they know the answers or need none will find the things they need to ask
    grow
ever the more urgent; and those who remain indifferent, oh,
these are the worst, in every way more heathen than those who have
    sinned.
It is far better to be scorned than ignored, but I would rather be loved,
not for having done anything wonderful, but simply for having tried to
    show
that there *are* ways of loving not beholden to longings attained;
that there are halcyon omens forever airborne, warm in the coldest
    wind.
And this one thing I'm certain of – that if ever the sea, or man, or ship,
were utterly shut down, not one of them, no, not one, can ever again
    restart.

Glossary

algorithm   A set of rules to solve a particular problem.
ampersand   The symbol "&" meaning "and".
apodixis   A clear demonstration.
avatar   A manifestation or incarnation; used in cyberspace as a symbol for oneself.
axon   Long appendage of a nerve cell, carrying signals.
baud   Bit-per-second; measurement of the speed by which information can be conveyed by a modem over the telephone line.
benthos   Flora and fauna found at the bottom of ocean or lake.
bitmapped   (A screen image) made up of tiny dots (pixels).
cyber   From "cybernation", control by machines. Used in "cyberspace" and "Cyberia" to describe the Internet.
emoticons   Small pictorial or abstract images to convey emotions in e-mail.
ergonomics   The study of the human-and-machine relationship.
fatbit   Graphic screen images blown-up to make them easier to work with.
fractal   Fractionally proportional; a circular equation which reproduces its own (irregular) pattern in larger or smaller forms.
grayscale   Gradable at all levels between black and white.
grok   Understand, understanding.
handsels   Gifts or foretastes.
hologram   = two- or three-dimensional image produced by light-beams.
kairos   Opportune and decisive moments (= orgasms).
kerning   The process of adjusting the spacing between letters or characters.
mandala   Symbolic circular figure representing a dreamer's search for self-perfection.
munge   A word derived from "mash until no good", meaning "destroy".
paradigm   A model, standard, pattern, ideal or paragon.
pixel   A compound of picture element. The smallest element or spot

	possible on a computer screen.
phasmanise	This and other italicized words and phrases in the same section are anagrams of "seamanship".
selectric	From the Selectric Typewriter – IBM's 1964 automatic word-processor.
sholes	A deliberate pun on "shoals". Christopher Sholes was the American who invented the typewriter.
telekineses	Movements far distant from their motive cause.
thalassa	Greek for "sea"; "thalassinos" is "a seafarer".
torus	A three-dimensional shape.

Some new and recent poetry from Anvil

PETER DALE
Under the Breath

DICK DAVIS
Belonging

HARRY GUEST
A Puzzling Harvest
COLLECTED POEMS 1955–2000

MICHAEL HAMBURGER
From a Diary of Non-Events

JAMES HARPUR
Oracle Bones

PHILIP HOLMES
Lighting the Steps

ANTHONY HOWELL
Dancers in Daylight

A B JACKSON
Fire Stations

MATTHEW MEAD
Walking Out of the World

E A MARKHAM
A Rough Climate

SALLY PURCELL
Collected Poems

GRETA STODDART
At Home in the Dark

JULIAN TURNER
Crossing the Outskirts

DANIEL WEISSBORT
Letters to Ted